Vic,

Life [illegible] mes,
but it sucks less when you
have good friends! I'm
here for you if you need!
If not, I'm here to have
a drink!. LOL

THE 5-MINUTE SELF-CARE JOURNAL FOR WOMEN

♡ Holly

P.S.
I'm totally
a dork!

The 5-Minute SELF-CARE JOURNAL for Women

Prompts, Practices, and Affirmations to Prioritize You

JUDITH BELMONT, MS

ROCKRIDGE PRESS

Interior and Cover Designer: Irene Vandervoort
Art Producer: Janice Ackerman
Editor: Carolyn Abate
Production Editor: Nora Milman
Production Manager: Eric Pier-Hocking

© Maria Galybina/Creative Market

Paperback ISBN: 978-1-63878-118-9
R0

THIS JOURNAL BELONGS TO:

La Victoria

Don't let anyone
treat you like a
yellow Starburst. You
are a Pink Starburst!

INTRODUCTION

Welcome to your self-care journey! I am so pleased you chose this book to improve yourself and your life. This book will provide support and guidance to nourish and encourage you as you make your self-care a priority. Consider this book like a self-care toolkit, offering important practical tips and strategies that you can use immediately to improve health and wellness in all areas of your life. The insights and practices will provide room for reflection and skill building as you make time for *you*.

By beginning this book, you have taken an important first step in committing to take five minutes a day for reflection and self-improvement. Setting aside time for ourselves is not an easy task while we juggle various life roles and responsibilities. What makes committing to self-care even more difficult is the unhealthy messages that many women have received early on in their lives that self-care is selfish and that selflessness is a virtue. This destructive message that we are not as important as others, along with the notion that attending to our needs is self-indulgent, is a major barrier to turning inward and allowing ourselves to focus on self-care.

Be assured that self-care is not only important for you to improve your mental, physical, and spiritual health, but it will also benefit those around you. The healthier you are, the healthier you will be for others. As you work on nourishing yourself and improving your coping skills, mastering your moods, thinking more rationally, and choosing self-compassion over self-judgment, you will be better equipped to manage your stress effectively and therefore will be healthier in your relationships. It's hard to give others what you don't even give to yourself. Indeed, working on yourself will be the best gift you can give to those around you.

As a retired psychotherapist and presently a mental health coach, as well as wellness trainer, speaker, and author of 10 books in the self-help/mental health field, I have seen the importance of self-care firsthand. My clients' ability to cope with daily stresses suffered when they put themselves on the back burner. In trying to be everything for everyone, way too many women seek help only after too many years of feeling anxious and burned-out as they tried to please others at the expense of themselves. Ironically, when they neglected their own self-care needs, their relationships with others close to them suffered, too. I have also seen that as my clients prioritized themselves and learned practices of self-care, their relationships and lives improved significantly.

I personally have experienced the importance of addressing my own self-care to be the best person I could be. When I have not addressed my own needs—found myself rushing instead of being mindful, spreading myself too thin—I lacked patience and calm with those close to me. The more I worked on my own self-care, the better I was for everyone. Positive energy is contagious. Happiness is contagious. Loving kindness is contagious.

Of course, this journal is not a substitute for professional help. If you find yourself experiencing anxiety, depression, or other mental health symptoms that are interfering with your

ability to cope in your daily life, the choice to seek help is courageous. This journal can be an adjunct to therapy to work through
complicated thoughts and feelings, but it is not a substitute for
professional help.

Thank you for joining me on this journey to be the best *you*
that you can be. Once you commit to make time for yourself,
you'll reap rewards that will improve your life.

HOW TO USE THIS BOOK

Making the commitment to set aside even five minutes a day will provide you with the support and structure you need to make major changes in your life.

This book has 150 five-minute entries, each providing prompts for reflection, space for journaling, a short practice, and an affirmation. All of these elements are designed to address various aspects of self-care to help you recommit yourself to nurturing your mind, body, and spirit. Of course, on days when you have more time, you can benefit from spending extra moments in reflection and journaling beyond the space provided.

Journaling has been found to have many health and wellness benefits. It provides an outlet for self-expression and exploration. It's also linked to boosting your physical health by strengthening the immune response and lowering blood pressure by decreasing stress.

Self-care is very personal—we all have different ways to nurture and take care of ourselves. One size does not fit all. Feel free to skip some entries that may not seem right for you, while spending more time on ones that do. Be sure to revisit relevant entries from time to time to help solidify your learning and facilitate your self-care growth.

May the prompts, practices, and affirmations help you take better care of a very special person in your life—*you*!

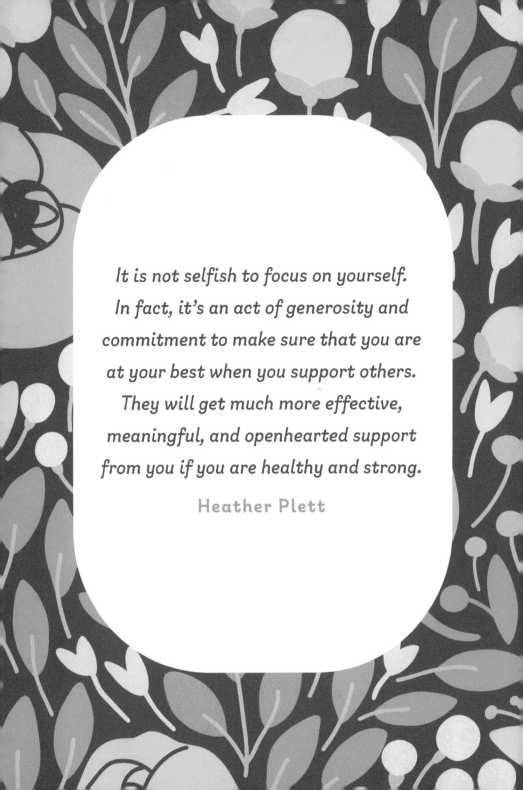

It is not selfish to focus on yourself. In fact, it's an act of generosity and commitment to make sure that you are at your best when you support others. They will get much more effective, meaningful, and openhearted support from you if you are healthy and strong.

Heather Plett

Reflect on Your Goals

You chose this journal to boost your self-care, so let's start off by exploring that decision a bit more. What areas of self-care have been difficult for you? In what areas of self-care do you want to improve?

....

....

....

....

....

....

Look at your list of answers and think about how to revise each challenge into a goal.

EXAMPLE:

CHALLENGE: "I have a hard time setting limits and saying 'no' because I'm afraid of being seen as selfish."

GOAL: "I want to develop my assertive skills to set limits without feeling guilty and stay true to myself."

———

Making my challenges into goals will help me move forward with optimism for the future.

Read and Write for Self-Care

Journaling helps you crystallize your thoughts, explore feelings and reactions, create opportunities to self-reflect, commit to goals, and keep track of your growth. How have journaling and reading been helpful in the past in making time for yourself?

_____

_____

_____

_____

_____

_____

_____

_____

Commit to devoting at least five minutes of journaling a day to help you establish lifelong habits of nurturing yourself. Use this book as a springboard for daily focus on your self-care journey, keeping track of your growth that will ideally continue to last a lifetime. Playing soothing music for your five-minute self-care practice will help set the stage for self-reflection.

———

Journaling, reading, and doing short practices will all help improve my self-care.

Affirmations Create Hope

Affirmations are positive and reassuring self-statements that help you overcome negative self-talk. Examples include "I love myself and accept myself unconditionally" and "I learn from my mistakes and keep on improving." What are some affirmations that can help you stop self-sabotaging, while offering you hope and support in good and bad times?

_____

_____

_____

_____

_____

_____

_____

Look at your list. Write down or print out a list of your affirmations. Place them in a bowl or box. Read one affirmation every day to stay positively focused.

———————————

I am a beautiful person, flaws and all.

Commit to Daily Self-Care

In our busy lives, it is hard to commit to reflection and introspection about self-care. Write down some of the advantages of making a commitment to prioritizing self-care.

_____

_____

_____

_____

_____

_____

_____

_____

_____

_____

Give yourself at least five minutes a day for your self-care journey. Create a self-care ritual such as setting aside time for using this book upon waking up, when sipping your morning drink, or before going to bed.

———————

I commit to making self-care a priority.

Start the Day with a Positive Intention

Positive intentions are self-care reminders that guide you to improved self-awareness. They help distance you from persistent negative thoughts. Think of a few phrases to keep ready when intrusive or negative thoughts bubble up.

EXAMPLES:

"I intend to be grateful today for everything in my life."

"I will focus on being kind to everyone I meet."

....

....

....

....

....

Make sure your intention is a positive one, not a judgmental one such as "stop being so sensitive." Set an alarm each morning to remind you to say your intention to yourself.

———————

My positive intention for today is to love and accept myself, even with my shortcomings.

Add Movement to Your Positive Intentions

Adding a gesture or movement to your positive intention ritual can make a stronger imprint on your brain. A yoga pose or cupping your hands as if you're holding your intention are a few examples. Write about a few movements you would like to try when you set your positive intention.

_____

_____

_____

_____

_____

_____

_____

_____

_____

_____

Review your list and identify one movement you'd like to try this week. Stick with it and do it every day as you set your intentions.

Using movement helps me experience positive intention with my body and mind.

An Act of Self-Love

One of the biggest obstacles to working on self-care is the message that it's a selfish act. Unless you live apart from mainstream society, selflessness is not a virtue. What's more, selflessness works against any efforts of self-care. What messages have you received about making self-care a priority that undermined your self-care focus?

_____

_____

_____

_____

_____

_____

_____

Challenge any responses above with a more rational alternative, supporting your right to regard self-care as a crucial step toward loving yourself.

Self-care is not selfish—
it is an act of self-love.

Take Care of Yourself

You are reminded when flying to put your own mask on first before helping others. List ways you need to take care of yourself so you can be better for others, too!

_____

_____

_____

_____

_____

_____

_____

_____

_____

Today, choose one goal to put into action by making it a **SMART GOAL**. SMART is an acronym for goals that are Specific, Measurable, Action-oriented, Realistic (or Relevant), and Time-bound.

———

I will make myself a priority and am committed to achieving my goals.

Self-Care Inventory

Self-care extends to many areas in your life, including your mental, emotional, physical, vocational, medical, financial, social, and spiritual well-being. Write about how you plan to take care of yourself in one of these areas.

_____

_____

_____

_____

_____

_____

_____

_____

From your list, identify areas that need more focus. Choose one thing today that you can do in a few of those areas to improve your self-care habits. For example, to attend to your physical self-care, start an exercise log to help motivate you and track your progress.

Many areas of my life could benefit
from my attention to self-care.

Create a Calming Space

Designating a calm, special place for self-reflection will be helpful in reading and writing for your five minutes of daily self-care. What spaces in your home do you find calming or soothing? Write about them.

_____

_____

_____

_____

_____

_____

_____

_____

_____

Find ways to make these spaces more conducive to your "me time." Add artwork, pictures of loved ones or beautiful scenery, framed quotes, or any special items that evoke positive feelings.

————————

Having a safe haven gives me a space to get in touch with my innermost thoughts and feelings.

Remind Yourself of Your Worth

Never doubt for a moment your self-worth. You are just as worthy now as when you were a beautiful, helpless baby coming into this world. Have you doubted your worth and put conditions on it? Write about your thoughts.

Take out a dollar bill of any denomination. Do anything you want to it so long as you keep it intact. Crumple it, stomp on it, crease it, fold it, and now unfold it again. After you straighten it out, ask yourself, "how much is it worth?" Of course, its value remains the same as does your value, no matter how worn or stepped on you feel.

I am worthy no matter what,
with no preconditions.

Love Yourself First

Self-love is often hard for people, as we are more likely to focus on our shortcomings and our flaws. However, loving yourself is the basis of self-esteem and the foundation of loving anything and everything else in your life. Take a few moments to reflect on what you really love about yourself.

_____

_____

_____

_____

_____

_____

_____

_____

Read your list of responses out loud and add more to it. Ask those around you what they find lovable about you to get some ideas. Looking at photos of yourself can help brainstorm ideas of loving attributes about yourself. If loving yourself is challenging, take the point of view of a supportive friend or family member.

———————

The more I love myself, the healthier my loving relationships will be with others.

You Have a Choice

Perhaps one of the best ways to take care of yourself is to recognize the importance and power of the choices you have in your life. All too often, we relinquish control of our lives to others and circumstances outside of ourselves. In what ways have you felt stuck in the belief that your actions, reactions, and even your attitudes are out of your control?

_____

_____

_____

_____

_____

_____

Today, remind yourself about the power of choice throughout the day, and strive today to choose well. Choose your attitude, choose your reactions, choose to get back up, choose to learn from setbacks, choose to take responsibility. Choose to focus on what you can change, not what you can't.

———

*The power of choice will determine
how my life turns out.*

Break Down Your To-Do List

We often have so much to do in our waking hours that we feel overwhelmed, which can lead to inaction. Think of some tasks on your to-do list that seem daunting and complex.

_____

_____

_____

_____

_____

_____

_____

_____

On a separate page and using your to-do list as a starting point, break down those daunting tasks into small chunks. Make sure that each task will only take five minutes.

———

Breaking down big tasks helps motivate me to tackle things one day at a time.

DATE:

Make Small Self-Care Goals

Too often we put conditions on our happiness. "I'll be happier when I lose 10 pounds . . . find that special someone . . . get a different job." These thoughts can prevent you from making small steps toward a bigger self-care goal. Think about some small steps you can take toward your goals.

_____

_____

_____

_____

_____

_____

_____

How can you find time to achieve your daily self-care goals? Write down a plan for using those steps to achieve your end goal. Strive to enjoy the process until you achieve your goal.

———

I commit to enjoying the steps and the journey to self-care without putting my happiness on hold any longer.

Spiritual Self-Care

You do not have to be religious to believe in a higher purpose. What are ways that you seek meaning in your life? What helps you derive a sense of purpose and commitment to a spiritual connection larger than yourself?

Identify your underlying values that make your life meaningful. Reading an inspirational passage each morning, whether it be a prayer, devotion, affirmation, or positive intention, can access a deeper meaning to your life.

---

*My spiritual self-care allows me
to seek meaning in my life.*

Stress for Success

Stressed spelled backward is *desserts*. It's an uncanny coincidence. It just shows how stress can be sweet! Stress can be a source of fulfillment and motivation. Write about how stress has been motivating and has spiced up your life. Managing stress is an important part of self-care as it is through stress that we grow and evolve.

_____

_____

_____

_____

When you think of managing stress, think of the 5 Cs of stress resilience:

CONTROL: Having a sense of control makes stress work for you.

COMMITMENT: When your stress has meaning for a higher purpose, it can be positive.

CONNECTION: Having social support helps us be more resilient.

CHALLENGE: See obstacles as challenges to overcome and a chance to grow.

CREATIVITY: Stress makes you more creative, since you need to think of new ways out of old problems.

---

*I embrace stress as necessary on
the path to my success.*

Find Quotes That Inspire

Quotations can help us nurture ourselves, offer comfort and support, and even inspire positive living. What quotations have inspired you? Why do you find those quotations meaningful?

Assemble the quotations that are meaningful to you. Print or write them out, cut them into strips, and put them in a container. Post them in prominent places in your living space or work space. Focus on one quote each day for inspiration, motivation, and validation.

Quotations can help nurture and support me.

DATE:

Choose Optimism

Optimism is a way of thinking that shows hope and confidence that things look bright for your future. It doesn't deny the reality of difficulties in your life; even when things go horribly wrong, you still have the belief things will turn out OK. Think about how you react throughout your day. Are you a pessimist or an optimist? Why?

There are many tools to help increase optimistic thinking. Positive intentions, affirmations, inspirational quotes, and mindfulness exercises are just a few ways to increase your optimistic attitude. Choose one to focus on and watch your optimism boost!

Optimism is a choice—I will focus on how I can learn and grow from any experience.

Strive for Authenticity, Not Perfection

Perfectionism is one of the greatest thieves of self-care. It robs you of self-esteem and tricks you into thinking you are only good enough if you meet certain standards. Reflect here on how perfectionism has hindered you rather than helped you.

....

....

....

....

Review your responses and reframe them with authenticity. What would your thoughts, actions, and feelings seem like if you strove for authenticity instead of perfection?

EXAMPLE:

PERFECTIONISTIC STATEMENT: "I need to be 20 pounds thinner to feel good about myself."

ACCEPTING STATEMENT: "My weight does not need to change for me to feel good about myself. My commitment to eating wholesome foods, being active, and staying hydrated makes me feel strong and motivated."

———

Instead of being perfect,
I will strive to be authentic.

Stop the Comparison Game

Take a moment to think about what triggers you to compare yourself to others. Does someone's good fortune make you feel inadequate, envious, or sad? What people do you compare yourself to over and over again?

....

....

....

....

....

....

....

....

....

The next time you compare yourself to others and feel inadequate, think about what appeals to you about someone's life. Use that information as motivation to pursue similar goals in your own life.

My self-worth cannot be based on comparing myself to others.

Find Meaningful Work

Whether it's a job outside the home, raising a family, or volunteering, work can give us a sense of meaning and connection in our lives. Describe how you find meaning in your working roles and how you balance your responsibilities with your personal needs and goals. What are some challenges in balancing it all?

....

....

....

....

....

....

....

....

....

....

Challenge yourself to find meaning in your work by reframing the way you describe your job duties. For example, if you see yourself as "just a housewife," reframe your role as "caring for others."

———————————

*I will continue to seek meaning
and purpose in my work.*

Release Negativity

Negative thoughts undermine your ability to take care of your mental and emotional health. Persistent negative thinking leads to depression and anxiety. What are some persistent negative thoughts that are hard for you to shake, causing you to doubt yourself and your greatness?

....

....

....

....

....

....

....

....

Consciously slow down your breathing and imagine those negative thoughts written on the boxcars of a train, with you watching from a bridge. Imagine yourself releasing those negative thoughts to the passing train, watching them as they go out of sight.

I choose to note my negative thoughts,
rather than react to them.

Develop Hobbies and Interests

Hobbies and interests are great stress relievers and vehicles for "me time." Hobbies can help you unleash creativity. They can also help you connect with like-minded people who share the same interests, creating a sense of community. List any hobbies or interests that you find enjoyable and the connections you have made through them.

Once a week, commit to partaking in a hobby or interest. Play tennis with a friend or explore local offerings in your community. Watch a YouTube video to get you started. Resolve to make time for your hobbies, even if you incorporate them a little at a time.

When I commit more time for my interests
and hobbies, I am saying yes to myself.

Hobbies as a Form of Play and Creativity

Hobbies should not put more pressure on you—the goal is stress relief and enjoyment, not perfection. Think about any hobbies you haven't pursued out of fear of not doing them well. What messages hold you back from pursuing things that interest you?

_____

_____

_____

_____

_____

_____

_____

Let yourself try new things even if you do not think you are good at them. Let creativity take over. Get out of your comfort zone and have fun!

———————

My hobbies offer me an enjoyable creative outlet, a form of play, and great stress relief.

Say No to Say Yes

All too often, when we end up saying *yes* to others it means saying *no* to ourselves. What are some people and situations you need to say *no* to so you can say *yes* to yourself?

_____

_____

_____

_____

_____

_____

_____

_____

_____

_____

What limits can you make today to say *yes* to yourself even if it means *no* to something else? Think of one limit you can set today and practice it, even if it means just practicing in front of the mirror.

———————————

I will not focus on pleasing people
at the expense of myself.

Meditative Walking

Walking and meditating are great ways to relax and support self-care. What are one or two short phrases (one or two words only) that are calming to you?

Spend a few minutes walking in place, around your living space or outside, and with each step think of the word or phrase of your choice. Keep repeating the same word or phrase for a few minutes, focusing on slowing your breath and on the calming words.

Meditative walking is calming and helps me slow my life down and focus on the positive.

Stretch It Out

Stretching has many benefits to keep your body in shape and calm your mind. Think about what you'd like to include in a regular stretching routine. Create a list of different stretching techniques that can become a part of your self-care.

_____

_____

_____

_____

_____

_____

_____

_____

Review your list and spend a few minutes completing the stretching techniques that you wrote down. Turn on some calming music or sit outside in the sun, if possible. Stretch all parts of your body while breathing slow, deep breaths, staying in touch with your body sensations.

Stretching will help energize my body and mind.

Take Time to Reflect

It's important to check in with yourself every now and then—particularly if you're working on creating new self-care habits with the help of this book. Take a few moments and reflect on how you are feeling, what you are thinking, and the sensations you're experiencing right now.

_____

_____

_____

_____

_____

_____

_____

_____

_____

Remind yourself that you are a "human being" and not a "human doing." Making this a frequent practice will help you feel centered and in touch with yourself.

Reflection gives me the space I need to nurture myself and be in touch with myself.

Turn Problems into Possibilities

Being able to solve old problems with new solutions is a form of self-care. What problems keep you stuck in negativity, confusion, and a sense of powerlessness? What roadblocks do you hit when you try to solve your problems? Write about what you would like to resolve once and for all.

Use reframing to turn problems into possibilities. When you do, you take control of your life back. For example, "I have few friends" can be turned into "It is possible to make more friends by joining interest groups and initiating conversations."

Possibility thinking offers me a fresh
way to look at old problems.

Seek Support

Having a strong sense of social support is an important ingredient to life satisfaction and resilience. Conversely, isolation and loneliness are linked to depression and unhappiness. What is the quality of your support system? What changes (if any) would you like to make in your support system?

_____

_____

_____

_____

_____

_____

_____

Be receptive to making a new friend or a new connection. Give someone a call, send someone a text, or make plans with a friend you haven't seen in a while.

———

Seeking social support will be a priority
in helping me combat isolation.

Heal Your Past

Perhaps the most important focus to emotional self-care is to heal from your past hurt and pain. These can range from small disappointments to deep trauma. What events from the past still hurt or affect you to this day? What past hurt or trauma can help explain your emotional triggers and negative thoughts that continue to show up?

_____

_____

_____

_____

_____

_____

_____

Read over your responses. Begin to prioritize treating yourself compassionately. Forgive yourself for any past actions you regret. Forgive others for not being able to give you what they did not have to give. Use gentle self-talk that is loving and accepting.

———

I will heal by being loving and gentle with myself.

Ask for Help

One of the best ways to take care of yourself is to allow others to help you heal and grow. Who do you go to, to seek help and support? What gets in the way of opening up and seeking the support that you need?

....

....

....

....

....

....

....

....

....

....

Today, enlist any help you might need, share something about yourself with someone you trust, or make an action plan to get support.

------

*I strive to become more open with
others instead of shutting down.*

Operate from a Place of Love

When we come from a place of love and open our hearts, we reap the benefits of building resiliency, compassion, and empathy for others. What loving thoughts first come to mind right now in this moment? What people or things are your loving thoughts directed to?

....

....

....

....

....

....

....

....

Express your feelings of love to others close to you—whether it be in a text, email, or in person. For everyone you interact with today, strive to show love and kindness through your expressions, smile, and behaviors. Say a kind word, offer a supportive gesture, give a hug.

———————————

Love is the key to uplifting my heart and my life.

Reprioritize Your Time and Energy

How you spend your day? Do you spend too much time doing things that you don't want to do? Do you have enough time and energy to do the things you really want? Reflect on where you spend your time.

Prioritize spending more time focusing on areas in your life you want to improve. Prioritize who you want to spend time with, too. Listing the pros and cons of your choices might help you prioritize.

As my needs change, I reprioritize what works for me.

Seek Meaning for Spiritual Self-Care

A cornerstone of spiritual self-care is the search for meaning and a sense of having a purpose. Those who find meaning in their lives tend to be more optimistic and resilient. What are the most meaningful things in your life? Your friends, family? Maybe your job or your pet? Write about the things that come to mind.

....

....

....

....

....

Look for the sense of purpose and meaning behind the scenes of your daily life—whether it means consciously committing yourself to finding more meaning in your work, joining a faith-based group, volunteering for a cause, spending more time in nature, or using prayer or meditation to facilitate reflection. Carve out a few hours this week to focus on things that are meaningful.

When I pursue what I find meaningful,
I feel more at peace.

Wrong Turns Can Bring You to the Right Places

Think of some of the wrong turns you've made in your life that perhaps you wouldn't make today. Would you have gone to a different school? Moved to another city? Chosen a different career?

....

....

....

....

....

....

....

....

Look at your list and review where you are now in life. Reflect how those wrong turns may have brought you to the right places.

Turn wrong turns into "right" turns.

DATE:

Develop a Self-Care Activity List

What does a self-care practice look like to you? It can be as simple as deep breathing, snuggling in a blanket, going outside and looking up at the sky, writing out your thoughts and feelings, or listening to or singing a favorite song. What are some activities that work for you that you find enjoyable?

_____

_____

_____

_____

_____

_____

_____

_____

_____

Use this list to remind you of how to regulate your emotions and stress during times when you need extra self-care help and support. Continue to add to your list.

Developing an evolving menu of self-care activities is a way of taking care of myself.

Don't Sell Yourself Short

It seems to be human nature that we focus on what we are doing wrong instead of acknowledging what we are doing right. Take a few minutes to consider the things that you have done right in the last day.

_____

_____

_____

_____

_____

_____

_____

Think for a moment about what you do right every day that you take for granted. For example, perhaps you were late to make dinner because you were fixing bikes in your garage for a family ride the next day. Appreciate that you have the skills to get the bikes into shape rather than focusing on your failure to prepare a timely meal.

———

I will stop taking what I do right for granted, appreciating instead my uniqueness and strengths.

Look Your Best

Looking your best is a form of self-care. It says to the world that you take time for you and that you matter. Reflect on what makes you feel like you look your best. List some important factors in looking your best.

_____

_____

_____

_____

_____

_____

_____

_____

_____

The one universal factor in looking your best is adding a smile. A smile helps you appear welcoming, kind, and positive. Take a minute to look in the mirror and smile. What do you convey with your smile? A smile is the best thing you can ever wear—and it looks so good on you! Try it today!

———————

A smile is the most important thing I can ever wear.

Create Balance

Creating life balance is one of the most important elements of self-care. How do you divide your time? This includes work, family, exercise, spirituality, friendships, volunteering, and childcare. Write down how you divide your time throughout the day or week.

_____

_____

_____

_____

_____

_____

_____

_____

On a separate piece of paper, draw two circles. In the first one, draw sections like a pie chart, depicting how you spend your time. In the other circle, draw the ideal pie chart of your life. Reflect on how they're different and where you can make change.

I strive to find more balance in my life.

Create a Personal Slogan

Think of a personal slogan that stands for the essence of who you are or what you believe in—a saying to help you stay on track. Repeating your slogan often can be meditative and soothing.

EXAMPLES:

"My positive thoughts will bring me to positive places."

"I believe in myself and my worth."

What personal slogans would work for you?

....

....

....

....

....

....

....

Use mantras in your self-care toolkit. Choose one of the slogans you listed today and write it on a sticky note or use it as a screen saver. Repeat your chosen slogan or mantra often throughout your day.

————————————

Personal mantras will help me stay on track to pursue my goals with confidence and support.

Be Aware of Negative Self-Talk

When you feel your self-esteem take a dip, watch out for negative self-talk that is critical and judgmental. What are some negative things you say to yourself that erode your self-confidence?

Looking at the list you made of critical self-statements, reframe each thought into a more compassionate and kinder thought. For example, "I failed in my most important relationships" can be changed to "I've had a hard time maintaining healthy relationships and have learned a lot to improve moving forward."

I strive to treat myself with only kindness and support.

Compare Yourself to Yourself

One of the biggest robbers of self-esteem is comparing yourself with others. In what ways do you compare yourself with others and find that you fall short? Give examples here.

....

....

....

....

....

....

....

....

....

....

....

....

Think for a few moments of how you've grown in the recent past. Do this practice daily to keep tabs on how you are growing into a heathier you.

———

I learn from others, but I will no longer compare myself to others. My self-esteem depends on it!

Don't "Should" Yourself

Do any of these statements sound familiar to you? *"I should be thinner," "I shouldn't have done or said that,"* or *"I should never have taken that job."* When you "should" yourself, you are eroding your confidence and undermining your emotional self-care. In the space provided, list the "shoulds" you impose on yourself that are self-critical.

_____

_____

_____

_____

Looking at your list of "shoulds," replace them with healthier, less judgmental language that shows a preference, not an absolute. Use these examples as your guide to write your own.

"SHOULDS"	PREFERENCE
"I should be better at making friends."	*"I would like to be better at making friends."*
"I shouldn't have done or said that."	*"I am sorry I did or said that."*
"I should never have taken that job."	*"The job did not turn out as expected."*

I will stop "shoulding" myself. Self-acceptance is an important part of self-care.

Keep Hope Alive with Temporary Thinking

Hope is the antidote to grief, sadness, and depression. Keeping hope alive is sometimes very hard to do when you are beset with trauma, grief, and loss. Write here what makes it hard to be hopeful sometimes.

_____

_____

_____

_____

_____

_____

_____

One way to keep hope alive is to differentiate between feelings and thoughts that are temporary rather than permanent. When you begin to feel knocked around or down, subtle shifts in language can make a difference in your outlook. Compare "Life is too difficult" to "Life feels very difficult right now."

———

As long as the sun rises, there is hope.

Give Yourself a Stress Break

Even in your busy and stressful day, do you take a stress break now and again? You can play a game of solitaire on your computer, read an article online, or close your eyes for a few minutes and be conscious of your breathing. What do you want to include in your daily stress break?

_____

_____

_____

_____

_____

_____

_____

_____

Set a timer on your phone this week to take a mini stress break each day—5 minutes. Use your list for ideas.

---

*I have control over giving myself
some space when I need it.*

Be Aware of What You Eat

Most of us are well informed about the basics of good nutrition, but often choose convenient foods that are high in fats and sugar. Do you tend to seek food for comfort too often? Do you use food as a panacea for boredom and negative moods? Reflect on your relationship with food and the choices you make.

_____

_____

_____

_____

_____

_____

_____

_____

An important aspect of nutritional self-care is first becoming more attentive to what you eat. Today, be more mindful of what you eat and start a meal log. Write down everything you eat for the next few days and the mood that you felt while you were eating. Keep the log for a few weeks and reflect on any trends or correlations.

I will be more conscious of the foods I eat and the triggers that affect my choices.

Improve on Yesterday

The mindset to *improve* yourself, rather than *prove* yourself, allows you to measure your progress against yourself rather than someone else's yardstick. Think about yesterday and reflect on how you could have improved your reactions or responses to challenging situations.

_____

_____

_____

_____

_____

_____

_____

Choose a goal for the day that will allow you to improve upon something from yesterday. Perhaps you had a difficult conversation with your boss that went nowhere, or maybe you didn't really push yourself during a workout. Commit to improving yourself on your own terms.

———————————

Instead of trying to prove myself to others, I will seek to improve myself from where I was yesterday.

Communicate Assertively

Honest and open expression of your thoughts, feelings, and needs is important to your social self-care. Take a moment to reflect on the thoughts or feelings that you have a hard time expressing with confidence and list them here.

....

....

....

....

....

Use "I" statements the next time you are struggling to express your feelings. They are hallmarks of healthy, confident communication. Starting with "I feel," "I think," or "I need" takes ownership of your thoughts and feelings.

ASSERTIVE: "I felt uncomfortable when you raised your voice at me."

AGGRESSIVE: "You made me upset when you raised your voice at me."

NONASSERTIVE: Says nothing to avoid conflict, suppressing anger.

———

I will choose to be assertive and honor my thoughts, feelings, and needs.

Check-In: Time to Review, Reflect, and Renew

In life, as in this self-care journal, take some time periodically to review things you have recently found helpful, what you have learned, and what you have found most challenging or most rewarding. Reflect on what has been the most meaningful for you.

_____

_____

_____

_____

_____

_____

_____

Your self-care journey will be most successful if you take the time to digest what you have learned and experienced. This goes not only for using this journal, but in life. Reflect and review periodically to take stock of your growth.

My growth is a choice
I make to take my self-care seriously.

Honor Your Feelings

In the last entry, you were asked to reflect, review, and renew. What feelings were triggered? Write about the feelings that were prompted by your reflections.

_____

_____

_____

_____

_____

_____

_____

_____

_____

_____

Visualize a gas light in your car. When fuel is low, the light on the dashboard goes on to let you know it's time to fill up. Honor your feelings like you would a gas light in your car.

––––––––––

Honoring my feelings is a way of honoring myself.

Have an Attitude of Gratitude

Spend a few moments asking yourself what you are grateful for. Write what first comes to mind.

....

....

....

....

....

....

....

....

....

....

Make gratitude a habit by thinking of at least three new things you're grateful for each morning when you wake up. This is perhaps one of the most important practices of self-care you can do.

———

Having an attitude of gratitude helps me choose positivity over bitterness.

Make a Box of Gratitude

How did it feel to identify three things you are grateful for in the last entry? What other rituals, habits, or practices can help you keep a grateful state of mind?

_____

_____

_____

_____

_____

_____

_____

_____

_____

_____

_____

_____

Write down three of your ideas on a notecard and place them in a box. Each morning, meditate on one or more of the prompts before you start your day. If there is a call to action, complete it.

I choose to be grateful for what I have,
rather than lament what I don't.

Get Better, Not Bitter

Now you're going to think of some of the most difficult challenges you are facing in the present or have faced in the past. Write these down in order from the most difficult to the least.

....

....

....

....

....

....

....

....

....

Look at your responses. For each challenge, think of one aspect that you are grateful for. What has the challenge taught you? How have you grown? How have the obstacles in your life made you a deeper, more empathetic person, for example?

I'm grateful for my obstacles; they help me grow.

Exhale Bitterness, Inhale Gratitude

What emotions did the last entry bring up? What were the challenges in finding a silver lining in any?

....

....

....

....

....

....

....

....

Look at your challenging thoughts. Close your eyes and inhale. When you exhale, imagine that you are breathing away a challenging thought you wrote down. Breathe in again, but this time replace that thought with an appreciation. For example, "I am bitter over the collapse of my marriage" can be replaced with a thought of gratitude such as, "I am grateful to be free to love again, this time a bit wiser."

———

I count my blessings, not my disappointments.

Focus on Your Medical Health

Take care of your body by having daily good health habits and seeking the help of professionals for regular medical care. How would you evaluate your medical self-care? What would you like to change?

....

....

....

....

....

....

....

....

Take one step today to take charge of your health. Make an appointment for a physical exam, dental cleaning, or dermatology checkup. Get up and take a walk or do yoga to improve your flexibility and fitness.

———

I take responsibility for my medical self-care, seeking help when I need it.

Making a Mosaic of Broken Dreams

Take a moment to reflect on any of your broken dreams and past hurts. Doing so helps you learn from your setbacks and disappointments and can lead to a brighter future.

....

....

....

....

....

....

....

Visualize your past hurts like broken pieces of your life that are made into a beautiful mosaic. Even with shattered dreams, we can make something beautiful—the wonder of a mosaic is that broken pieces can form something else even more beautiful than its earlier form. What pieces of your past disappointments can be made into something new and beautiful?

————————————

I will use my broken dreams as pieces of a mosaic and make my life more beautiful than ever.

DATE:

Trade Old Dreams for New Ones

Let's take this one step further and focus on trading old dreams for new ones. Write about your desires and hopes for your future and the dreams you have for yourself that fit you better now.

_____
_____
_____
_____
_____
_____
_____
_____

Use the same mosaic visualization again to make your new dreams a reality. Only this time, imagine the pieces of broken dreams transformed into stepping-stones on the path that moves forward in your life.

---

*I will use my old dreams as stepping-stones
to move toward my new dreams now.*

Celebrate Yourself

Time to celebrate yourself—not just your achievements and what you are proud of, but your efforts and your intentions. What are you proud of? Have you overcome adversity and grown stronger?

Give yourself extra time today to do something that makes you happy. Take a walk in a new setting, treat yourself to a special meal, buy yourself flowers, or write a congratulatory note to yourself. What would celebrating yourself look like for you?

I celebrate who I am and what I am becoming.

The Power of Music

Music is an important item in many people's self-care toolkits. It evokes powerful emotions and soothes in a way that words alone often can't. What are some of your favorite songs? Why are they special to you? How has music helped in good times and bad?

Listen to one of your favorite songs with mindful awareness. What feelings and sensations does the music evoke in you? Reflect how that feels. Make a commitment to listen to a favorite song every day or your favorite playlist once a week.

I am grateful for music, which helps evoke powerful emotions and memories.

DATE:

Dare to Be Vulnerable

Vulnerability allows us to grow and be authentically ourselves. That means taking chances to express our thoughts, feelings, and needs even if we leave ourselves emotionally vulnerable. What has it been like when you took chances to step out of your comfort zone to be more open and authentic? If a lack of confidence has held you back, what has that felt like?

_____

_____

_____

_____

_____

_____

_____

_____

The next time you feel yourself holding back during a conversation, remember what you wrote. Take a chance and express yourself in the moment.

I will be courageous and face my fears of vulnerability so I can be true to myself.

Coping with Failure

Failures are necessary on the path to success. What are some failures you have experienced? How have those failures affected you?

_____

_____

_____

_____

_____

_____

In history, there are many examples of successful people who experienced astounding failures. Look at each of your responses and turn each failure into a goal that will serve as a stepping-stone to your success.

EXAMPLE: "I failed at my marriage."

GOAL: "I am looking forward to bringing what I learned from my previous marriage into improving my close relationships in the future."

---

*I will use failures as a foundation
for my future success.*

Sleep Self-Care

Everyone has different sleep needs, but we all need enough sleep to feel restored and refreshed. If our sleep suffers, our mood suffers, too. What interferes with your sleep? What strategies do you use to get enough sleep?

....

....

....

....

....

....

....

Develop a routine or ritual, such as lighting incense or meditating, to help calm and relax you before bed. Keep track of which routines help. Write down how you feel or your mood, as well as when routines work versus when they don't work. Seek the help of a physician if you want to explore sleep aids.

——————————

Addressing my sleep needs is another step toward good self-care.

Take Relaxation Breaks

Taking time to unwind and using relaxation techniques are vital elements of self-care. What are ways that you relax your mind and body?

....

....

....

....

....

....

....

....

A body scan is an effective technique to relax your mind and body. While sitting or lying comfortably, take deep breaths from your belly and focus on each area of your body in turn. Concentrate on the sensations of each area and what that area does for you before going to the next.

Relaxation is good for my mind and body.

Live Life, Right Now

Keeping your mortality in mind can help you gain perspective on what is truly important. Write about choices you can make right now to help you live life to the fullest.

Estimate your life expectancy and use each inch on a measuring tape to correlate to a year of your life. How much remains? This is not meant to be depressing, but rather a reminder of how important it is to not take any days for granted and live life to the fullest. How can this perspective help you appreciate that the time is NOW to live more purposefully?

I strive to not sweat the small stuff and make choices to live more fully now.

Reading as a Self-Care Practice

Reading can contribute to a mentally healthy life and is an important strategy for self-care. It reduces stress and improves your writing, vocabulary, and thinking skills. What are some of your favorite books, magazines, or websites? How does reading help you take care of *you*?

_____

_____

_____

_____

_____

_____

_____

Carve out time each day to attend to your self-care reading needs. Join a book club, or start one yourself.

———————————

*Carving out time to read every day allows
me to learn, recharge, and de-stress.*

Embrace Your Imperfections

We all know theoretically that to be human is to be imperfect, but often we have a hard time accepting our mistakes, failures, and imperfections. Write about some of your imperfections that you presently struggle with accepting.

....

....

....

....

....

Looking at your responses, reflect on how you can replace perfectionism with a statement of acceptance.

EXAMPLES:

PERFECTIONISTIC STATEMENT: "I need to get excellent evaluations for my presentation, and if I don't I will feel like a failure."

ACCEPTING STATEMENT: "I will do my best to give an excellent presentation, but the evaluations of others do not determine my competence. I will do the best I can and learn from any negative comments or outcomes."

I am perfectly imperfect!

Get Moving!

What activities do you enjoy that get you moving and keep you active and energized?

Look at your list and commit to a regular exercise routine that you enjoy, even just for 15 to 20 minutes a day.

---

*I'm committed to regular physical activity
to keep myself healthy in mind and body.*

Create a Self-Care Kit

We are midway through this book. What tips and practices have you used the most often? What areas of self-care still need to receive more attention? List five of the most helpful insights and practices, including what you want to commit to working on.

_____

_____

_____

_____

_____

For at least three of these insights, think of an object to metaphorically represent each one. Seek out those items around your house and place them in a self-care toolkit (bag or box) to remind you of the most important lessons. For example, if you want to better manage your stress, put a stress ball in your kit. Consider adding to the kit regularly and put it in a prominent place to remind you about the importance of self-care.

Strategies such as a self-care toolkit will help me keep focused on working on my self-care.

Use Self-Compassion

We once thought that achievement was the way to self-esteem, but true self-esteem results from the ability to be kind to yourself, forgiving, and self-loving, no matter how many mistakes you make and how many times you fall short. What are ways you can be more self-compassionate?

_____

_____

_____

_____

_____

_____

_____

To boost self-compassion, touch your heart or give yourself a soothing massage in the area of your heart. Say comforting words to yourself such as, "May I be self-loving."

———

I choose self-compassion over self-judgment
and will accept myself unconditionally.

Choose Self-Kindness

Self-kindness is actually one of the most important self-care "musts" that underlies the ability to truly nurture yourself. Think of three ways that you can replace your negative self-talk with words of loving kindness to yourself and list them here.

....

....

....

....

....

....

....

....

The next time you're hard on yourself, imagine that a friend is saying harsh words (like the ones you hear in your head) to themself. Come back to what you wrote here and use these words to offer support and kindness to your "friend" (that is, you).

———————

I choose self-kindness over
self-criticism moving forward.

Create Unconditional Self-Love

Unconditional self-love underlies the foundation of self-care. If you do not love yourself, you will be less likely to make self-care a priority. What are ways that you love yourself? What gets in the way of truly loving yourself? How can you increase ways you show love to yourself, to improve self-care?

....

....

....

....

....

....

....

Take out a picture of yourself as a young child (or imagine it if you don't have one) and look at it closely. Is the child you see lovable and worthy? Despite the flaws and blemishes over time, you are still the same person and as beautiful and worthy as ever of that same love.

I choose to love myself without conditions.

Social Self-Care

To be human is to need other people. Seeking social support is a vital element in a self-care plan. All too often in times of stress, people choose to isolate themselves and shun support rather than seek it. What are you happy with about your social support system and what would you like to change?

....

....

....

....

....

....

....

....

Don't wait for people to come to you—reach out. Think of at least one person to reach out to today to make plans, share with them some challenges you are going through, or just let them know you are thinking of them.

I am working on increasing my circle of support by being more open with my thoughts and feelings.

Set Limits

Let's continue working on your social support circle. Reflect for a few moments on the quality of your relationships. Which people in your life respect your boundaries? Which don't? Write about both here.

_____

_____

_____

_____

_____

_____

_____

_____

Based on your reflections above, take steps to set limits with people who do not support your boundaries or growth. For example, speak your truth instead of saying what you think someone wants to hear.

———

Setting limits is an act of self-love and self-care.

Seek Support

Social support is vital to an emotionally balanced life. Isolation leads to loneliness and alienation. Who provides emotional support in your life? Who looks to you for social support?

_____

_____

_____

_____

_____

_____

_____

_____

_____

Recommit yourself to the relationships that support your growth and offer support, and protect yourself from relationships that do not. Find activities and interests to share with others, and always expand your network of support instead of shrinking it.

———

Seeking and giving support is a cornerstone of self-care.

Take A Mental Vacation

No matter what your life circumstances, you can always take mental vacations to offer some respite from daily stresses. Where would your go-to places be for a mental vacation break, even for a few minutes?

....

....

....

....

....

....

....

....

Sit down, close your eyes, and consciously slow your breathing. Imagine yourself in a place where you feel good and happy. Imagine sitting on the beach, listening to the sound of the waves, feeling the sand in your toes while smelling the ocean air. After taking a few moments, open your eyes refreshed, ready to take on the day.

*Giving myself mental vacations will
help me manage my stress.*

Take an Appreciation Break

Periodically taking stock of what you appreciate can help you focus on what is going right in your life and is a great way to lift your mood. What are some things that you appreciate right now?

_____

_____

_____

_____

_____

_____

_____

_____

_____

_____

Set a timer on your smartphone a couple times a day to remember to stop, breathe slowly, and appreciate. Be sure to bookmark this page so you can recite what you wrote during your "time-out."

_I am filled with appreciation for
the gifts I have in my life._

Refuse to Be a People-Pleaser

People-pleasing is more about your own lack of confidence and self-worth than valuing what others think. We all want to please others and be liked; the difference is that, when you are a people-pleaser, your self-esteem depends on it! Write about some examples of people-pleasing that you experience.

_____

_____

_____

_____

_____

_____

_____

Choose assertive communication instead of nonassertive people-pleasing. Use "I" statements that are direct and honest but tactful. A general formula for "I" statements is "I feel _____ when you _____." Practice using "I" statements by rehearsing in front of a mirror or with someone you trust.

I give up the desire to people-please and will focus instead on being pleased with myself.

DATE:

Give a Piece of Your Heart

One of the most important aspects of a close relationship is the ability to express and receive love. Your self-care depends on this important communication skill, because when you are connected to others, you are open to receiving and giving love that nourishes everyone involved. What are some ways that you show love to the most special people in your life?

....
....
....
....
....
....
....
....

Use the action items on your list throughout your day—and not just with the people you love. Minimize conflict in all areas of your life, whether they happen with coworkers, friends, or family. Give a piece of your heart, not your mind.

My heart is open to others without judgment.

Watch What You Say

The next time you find yourself wanting to shout out whatever words come to mind, think of a feather pillow that has exploded. Once the feathers are out, you can't get them all back. Think about those moments you said things you regret. How did those words affect your relationship with the other person? How can you grow from those experiences?

_____

_____

_____

_____

_____

_____

_____

Remember when you feel angry that *anger* is one letter short of *danger.* To cool down, take a long breath and don't react too quickly when you are distressed. Count to 10 or take a mindful minute.

I will be careful with what I say to avoid saying things I can't take back.

Identify Your Rights

Your basic human rights are a key component of your social self-care. List some rights that are difficult for you to accept, such as "I have a right to say *no*," "I have a right to make mistakes," or "I have a right to not be perfect."

....

....

....

....

....

....

....

....

....

....

Think of a relationship you have now in which one or more of the rights you value are not honored. Choose one right and take a stand for it in that relationship.

I have a right to act in a way that is best for me so long as it does not violate the rights of others.

Take a Nature Break

Reconnecting with nature is a superb form of self-care. Spend at least a few minutes out in nature, going for a walk, sitting out on your porch sipping your morning drink, or reading under a tree (if weather permits!). Enjoy the fresh air. How does it feel?

Nature is a great healer, but if you can't get outside and need a break, imagine sunlight radiating through you. Bask in the warmth and splendor.

Nature helps bring me back to a sense of wonder and calmness about the world.

Be Part of a Community

Ironically, getting involved in things outside of yourself is an act of self-care. Being part of a community can make you feel a sense of belonging. What are ways to engage more in support systems based on your interests and needs?

....

....

....

....

....

....

....

....

Meaningful actions and connections will help you feel engaged and involved. Join an interest group, a meet-up group, or find others who share common interests and spiritual practices. Involve yourself in issues that you believe in.

———

Finding a sense of community offers me
spiritual and emotional meaning.

Physical Self-Care Check-In

Our bodies give us signs when physical self-care needs more attention. For example, if your hands and feet are dry, make a plan to use skin cream after you bathe each day. If your back is stiff, think of a few stretching exercises you can do each day. Write down a few ideas.

_____

_____

_____

_____

_____

_____

_____

For the next few weeks, pay close attention to your physical self. In the morning, notice any aches and practice stretching to soothe the body. Do the same in the evening before bedtime.

———

*I commit to caring for my body to improve
my physical as well as mental health.*

Move Past the Past

Our focus on emotional self-care helps free us from the chains of the past. The past is a great place to visit, but you don't want to live there. What about the past is hard to move past?

_____

_____

_____

_____

_____

_____

_____

_____

Imagine the issues that you are stuck on from the past are on the front page of a newspaper. What is it about old news that keeps it on the front page at this point in your life? Reflect on how you can put these items, which are no longer so newsworthy except in your head, farther back in the paper. What news from your life do you choose to put on the front page now?

———————————

_I am no longer a hostage to a point in
time that cannot be changed._

Quote to Let Go of the Past

Inspirational quotations can help us get out of our invisible prisons and can set us free from being held back any longer. What quotations have been helpful to you? Or what words of wisdom have you heard that helped you move forward?

_____

_____

_____

_____

_____

_____

_____

_____

_____

Put your quotations on your screen saver or desktop notes, or write some on cards to carry with you for when you need them.

———

_Inspirational quotations help me
focus on moving forward._

Be Proactive

All too often, people wait for problems to occur before they take their health seriously. Reflect on your self-care habits to promote your health and prevent disease. What are some things you do to take care of your health?

_____

_____

_____

_____

_____

_____

_____

_____

_____

_____

Look at your answers. If you have been putting off making medical appointments or scheduling procedures, do it today. Join that gym! Make a to-do list today of proactive steps to make your health a priority.

I am proactive instead of reactive in my self-care.

Be Mindful

In our busy lives, where we often live too much inside our heads, immersing ourselves in the beauty of the present moment can be a challenge. Being mindful doesn't mean interrupting your daily life. Rather, it's a way of life. When you think of the term *mindfulness*, what words come to you?

_____

_____

_____

_____

_____

_____

_____

Look at your surroundings with what's called a "beginner's mind," as if you are seeing things for the first time. Look around with non-judgmental awareness. Be aware of your present sensations with all your five senses: sight, touch, smell, sound, and taste. What do you notice that you were not aware of even a few moments ago?

———

Mindful practice frees me from being a prisoner of my past and anxieties about my future.

Cultivate Mindfulness

With the fresh perspective of a beginner's mind, focus inward. Mindful awareness can help you be present-focused and free you from ruminating about the past and negative thoughts about the future. What are some ruminations you'd like to break away from?

_____

_____

_____

_____

_____

_____

_____

_____

Look at your list as if the statements were subtitles on a movie screen. Imagine yourself watching your thoughts from a distance. Defuse your mind from past or future worries by distancing and observing those disturbing thoughts.

———

I choose to observe my negative thoughts instead of ruminating about them.

Take a Mindful Moment

Let's try another exercise. Breathing deeply, inhaling through your mouth and slowly exhaling through your nose, take a moment to observe your surroundings. Give yourself a mindful moment. What do you notice? How does it feel to be mindful?

_____

_____

_____

_____

_____

_____

_____

_____

For the next week, start each morning with a 10- to 15-minute meditative practice. Look up a new practice online or use the example here.

---

*Mindful moments help me see that
my negative spin isn't fact.*

Mindfulness for Safety

Think of the last time you were preoccupied in your head and not conscious of your surroundings. What happened? Did you trip on the sidewalk? Misplace your phone or car keys?

_____

_____

_____

_____

_____

_____

_____

_____

Think of one thing you can do today to be more mindfully aware and spend a few moments practicing it. For example, as you take a walk, be mindful of the sidewalk's imperfections in order to avoid falls. As you go about your daily life, try to take at least a few moments to slow down, focus on your surroundings, and keep safe!

———————————

I am conscious of slowing down and being more mindful to keep myself safe and at peace.

You Are Special

You are special in many ways. All too often, we focus on our short-comings. How about focusing on your uniqueness? What makes you special? What are you proud of? List your responses.

_____

_____

_____

_____

_____

_____

_____

Take slow breaths, and remember what a miracle you are. Whatever happens in your day, keep in mind that you are lucky to be alive and meant to be here, and be amazed at your awesomeness. Think of yourself as a miracle; after all, the chances of you becoming yourself are slimmer than the odds of you becoming president of the United States!

———

I vow not to lose sight of the fact that I am special and unique.

Watch Out for Cognitive Distortions

Cognitive distortions are types of thinking errors that keep your mental narrative negative and self-critical. There are many types of cognitive distortions:

ALL-OR-NOTHING THINKING: "I always screw up."

FORTUNE-TELLING: "I'll never get over this."

JUMPING TO CONCLUSIONS: "He's mad at me—he must hate me!"

LABELING: "I'm unlikeable."

PERSONALIZATION: "They are making fun of me!"

Think of your own examples for each of the types of distortions.

....

....

....

....

When you have self-critical thoughts, write down each negative thought and its type of distortion. It can help you be more objective about your self-critical thoughts and teach you to recognize the distortions.

I identify my self-critical thoughts in order to think more rationally.

Replace Your Cognitive Distortions

How did it feel to explore your errors of thinking? Can you identify situations, people, or events that trigger your tendency to think in unhealthy ways?

_____

_____

_____

_____

Let's take this a step further and replace any distortions you have identified with more positive and factual self-statements. Use the examples below as a model.

SELF-CRITICAL THOUGHT	COGNITIVE DISTORTION	RATIONAL ALTERNATIVE
"I always screw up."	All-or-nothing thinking	"I am human and make mistakes."
"I will always be anxious."	Fortune-telling	"I can learn to control my anxiety."
"I'm lazy."	Labeling	"I feel unmotivated right now."

Finding rational alternatives to my distortions helps me quell my unhealthy self-talk.

Give Up Labels

People often distort their self-view through labeling. That's when one word or phrase is used to sum up your self-worth, such as "I'm an idiot" or "I'm a loser." This is cognitive distortion on life support! Labeling is also destructive and does considerable damage to your social self-care. What are the labels that come to mind that you use against yourself and others?

....

....

....

....

....

....

....

Looking at the list, imagine yourself relabeling the names you call yourself and others. Instead of "I'm an idiot," imagine putting an actual adhesive paper label over that word and finding a new, more comforting and factual word, such as "I am fallible."

---

*Giving up my tendency to label means
I am choosing empathy over criticism.*

DATE:

Shift from Victim Language to Victor Language

Blaming others for your feelings makes you a victim. When you take responsibility for your thoughts and feelings, you become the victor. For example, "He makes me mad" is victim language. "I was mad when he acted rude to me" shows you think like a victor. Write down examples of how you use victim language.

Today, be aware of when you're using these terms. Stop yourself and reframe what you're saying into victor language. Remember, you are in control of your feelings.

I am in control of my perceptions, reactions, and feelings.

Don't Believe Everything that You Think

Sometimes our minds create lies that we tell ourselves, which can make us feel bad. "I've been a bad parent"; "They're better than me"; or "I'm pathetic" are examples. But these lies are just stories, not facts—false narratives that aren't true. What untruths do you tell yourself that erode your healthy sense of self?

....

....

....

....

....

....

....

Looking at your list, think about an emotionally laden lie that you tell yourself and replace it with facts that are true. "I'm pathetic" can be replaced with a more factual "I am hurting and my self-confidence has dwindled." Replace each irrational thought on your list with a more factual alternative.

_____

I strive to separate fact from fiction and stop listening to any false narratives about myself.

Distance Yourself from Disturbing Thoughts

How did it feel in the last exercise to become more objective and less judgmental about your disturbing thoughts? What obstacles (if any) did you encounter while distancing yourself from your disturbing thoughts?

_____

_____

_____

_____

_____

_____

In this technique, you use visualizations to defuse disturbing thoughts in your mind. One way is to imagine that each judgmental thought is written on a cloud or on leaves in a stream, and to watch them slowly float away. Even a few moments using imagery like this will help you be more present, focused, and at peace.

———————

I will commit myself to practice looking at my thoughts rather than from my thoughts.

Give Yourself a Break

Take a few moments and some deep breaths and give yourself a break. Take some time to just breathe deeply and clear your head, or give yourself permission to stop ruminating about what can't be changed. How did that feel?

....

....

....

....

....

....

....

....

In times of stress and upset, remind yourself to take a break. Imagine a stop sign or use a timer on your phone to give yourself a daily "time-out."

I will give myself a "time-out" from stress when I need a break.

Take Belly Breaths

Slowing your breathing can help you in times of anxiety, emotional upset, and stress. As we slow our breathing, our hormones actually send messages to the brain to relax our fight-or-flight response. What types of breathing practices have helped you in times of stress?

....

....

....

....

....

....

To help you belly breathe, put one hand on your stomach and one hand on your chest. Usually, people take shallow breaths from their chests. Feel yourself now inflating your stomach to take a deep belly breath. Notice your hand raising up and then going down on each exhale. Breathe in through your mouth and exhale through your nose. If you are experiencing negative thoughts that increase stress, imagine them coming in and going out with each breath.

————

I belly breathe for peace of mind and calm.

What I Admire about Myself

A foundation of self-respect and self-acceptance is the basis for self-care. Reminding yourself of how special you are every day can help positively rewire your brain. Take an inventory of your strengths. Think of at least five things that you admire about yourself or are proud of.

....

....

....

....

....

....

....

....

....

Look at your list and give yourself a pat on the back. Look in the mirror and read it out loud and proudly. Take a picture of the list with your smartphone and look at it periodically to remind you of your strengths.

————————

I am proud of myself and worthy of admiration.

Slow Down

There is a time to multitask and a time to focus on only one thing at any given moment. For example, talking to your loved one while staring at the computer to get your work done might be more efficient, but it makes you less emotionally available to others. What can you do to slow down today?

_____

_____

_____

_____

_____

_____

_____

_____

Give yourself extra time for everything you do today. This allows you time to enjoy the moment and relax into your day.

When I slow down, I take time to savor
the moment and feel more centered.

Change "Have to" to "Want to"

What things do you feel you "have to" do today—such as cleaning the house, shopping for groceries, or going to work—as opposed to what you "want to" do? Write them down.

_____

_____

_____

_____

_____

_____

_____

_____

_____

Look at your "have to" list and come up with a new list that gives you more control. Focusing on what you choose to do offers a sense of self-empowerment. Practice this reframing as you go about your day.

Focusing on my sense of choice
makes me feel empowered.

Ask Yourself the Right Questions

Asking yourself questions is a way to prioritize your values and goals and honor your feelings and thoughts. Examples of the types of questions to ask yourself include, *"Am I living a life of meaning?"; "What things do I value most?"; and "What can I do to improve my self-care?"*

....

....

....

....

....

....

Avoid asking yourself rhetorical questions such as "How could I have done that?" or "How could I be so stupid?" They're really just put-downs disguised as questions. Think of some rhetorical questions you often ask yourself and revise them. For example, "How could I have done that?" can be changed to "What was triggered in me to cause me to react that way?"

Using open-ended questions instead of rhetorical questions helps me on my self-care journey.

Choose Your Reaction

Stress is in the eye of the beholder. What is stressful for one person may not be for another. Name some things in your life that are difficult and stressful.

....

....

....

....

....

....

....

....

Looking at your responses above, identify how you can adjust your self-talk so that you can change your stress reactions. For example, traffic itself does not stress you out directly—you are stressed *in response* to the enormous of number of cars moving slowly on the road.

———————

Things don't stress me out—I am stressed about them. I can choose my reaction.

Get Through It!

One important aspect of self-care in dealing with trauma or very difficult emotions is to limit unrealistic expectations that you must "snap out of it" or "get over it." Trauma, loss, and emotional or physical abuse might have lasting scars. However, that does not mean you cannot get through them. What are some things that you have found difficult to get over?

_____

_____

_____

_____

_____

_____

_____

Allow yourself the time you need to heal, without expecting yourself to get over it. Focus on your resiliency. Reflect on how you have become wiser and how your life was enriched by moving beyond the past with increased wisdom and insight.

———

For things I cannot really ever get over, I will strive to get through them with resiliency and wisdom.

Put Humor in Your Life

A good sense of humor is an important ingredient in self-care. Take a few moments to write how your life would be different if you could be lighter, see the humor in things, and laugh at life and other people's imperfections—as well as your own! In what ways would you like to "lighten up?"

....

....

....

....

....

....

....

....

Look for ways today to welcome more humor into your life. Laughter is good for the soul! Give yourself the ability to see new perspectives and the positive side of things. Today, make an effort to see the humorous side of life, and challenge yourself to find the bright side to everything that happens.

—————

I welcome laughter and humor in my life.

Forgive for Goodness' Sake!

Forgiveness is an important element in self-care. If we are held back by grudges and bitterness, we are the ones who pay. Sometimes it is hard to forgive those whose actions and words have been hurtful. Who do you have a hard time forgiving?

_____

_____

_____

_____

_____

_____

Looking at your responses, ask yourself these questions:

* *Am I keeping grudges?*

* *Is my lack of forgiveness robbing me of joy today?*

* *Have I become a prisoner of my past?*

* *Do I need to forgive life for not giving me what I had hoped it would?*

I choose to forgive in order to free myself from what I am powerless to change.

Forgive—But Don't Hang Around for More

Think of the people in your life who've caused you the most pain. Forgiving them may be hard, but it is a gift you can give yourself. To forgive is not to condone behavior, but to release yourself of the negativity and power they have over you. Build on yesterday's entry. Focus on one particular hurtful situation that affects you even today.

Writing a forgiveness letter to someone can be an important step in self-care. This letter is not meant to be sent. Rather, it is a vehicle for you to release yourself from the negativity of harboring a grudge. Explain in the letter why you need to set limits, even to the point of keeping the person out of your life. As you write, keep in mind that people can't give you what they don't have to give. It's easier to forgive if you see it that way.

I choose to forgive people who have hurt me, but I will not go back for more.

Heal from the Hurt

So, how did it feel to work on forgiving others—to free yourself of being held hostage to them emotionally? Is it hard not to rent out space in your head to others? Reflect on the feelings you have as you strive to let go of the anger and bitterness.

Visualize sitting by a stream or ocean and cupping your hands to hold your grudges, hurts, and bitterness. Imagine yourself slowly releasing your grasp so your fingers let out the negativity and hurt, surrendering it into the water, and watch it float away.

I surrender the bitterness that has held me back.

DATE:

Refuse to Collect Injustices

An important part of forgiveness is to give up the desire to hold on to how you were wronged. Refusing to be a collector of injustice is perhaps one of the most important steps to peace of mind and mental and emotional self-care. Using the previous prompt as an example, do you feel caught up in indignation over others who you perceive have slighted you? What injustices are you keeping on life support?

_____

_____

_____

_____

_____

_____

Even if you were in the right 100 percent, letting go of your anger is one the biggest gifts you can give to yourself. Today, think of one specific thing you can do or think about to shift your focus from collecting injustices to developing insight.

———

I refuse to focus on the unfairness of others and of life, as I only have control over my reaction.

Self-Forgiveness

It is not uncommon that we are hard on ourselves for mistakes, failures, and regrettable moments that we can't take back. In the space provided, write about a moment like this from your life.

_____

_____

_____

_____

_____

_____

_____

_____

_____

Reflect on things you have done that are hard to forgive. Resolve to forgive yourself; move from "why?" to "what's next?"

———

I forgive myself for not having the foresight to know what is now so obvious in hindsight.

Turn Regrets into Learning Experiences

Turning regrets into learning experiences is an important part of your emotional self-care. You can turn regrets around by focusing on what you learned from each negative experience. Write about some here.

....

....

....

....

....

....

....

Look at your responses and ask yourself, "What did I learn?" Reflect on how you can build on these lessons instead of being stuck on things you cannot change. Today, try to make your regrets productive rather than unproductive.

———

No matter what happened, I keep learning and growing and moving forward.

Positive Intentions

Think of a few positive self-care intentions that you can remind yourself of throughout the day to improve your mental, spiritual, or emotional health.

EXAMPLES:

"I intend to be grateful today for everything in my life."

"I will focus on being kind to everyone I meet."

For the next few weeks pick a positive intention for each day. Take it a step further and perform a ritual around your intention, such as cupping your hands and holding your intention.

My positive intention for today is to love and accept myself, even my shortcomings.

Use Visualizations for Self-Care

Visualizations use mental imagery. They help us gain insight as we use them to understand and master stressful feelings and thoughts. Visualizations can also help us develop confidence by allowing us to mentally rehearse situations that are challenging, such as giving a presentation to a room full of colleagues. What images do you see as helpful during a visualization exercise?

_____

_____

_____

_____

_____

_____

Visualize a storm right outside your home. Now imagine the storm passes and gives way to sunny skies. As you observe this, envision yourself as a weather reporter. Picture yourself reporting on the storm and then reporting on the calm after the storm. Even though we cannot control turbulence in our lives, we can choose to react calmly to it. Eventually, the storms in our lives will pass.

Visualizations help me move through challenging times with hope and confidence.

Inhale Positivity, Exhale Negativity

Imagine breathing in positivity and breathing out negativity. What negative thoughts come to mind that you would like to breathe out, and what positive thoughts would you like to welcome?

_____

_____

_____

_____

_____

_____

_____

Now spend a few moments belly breathing. Imagine that your breath is a color, and as you inhale, the color goes in your mouth and through your body to the extremities. As you exhale, envision the color moving from your extremities through your body and out through your nose. As the color you visualize is released with your breath, imagine letting go of negativity.

I breathe out negativity and breathe in positivity.

Allow Play into Your Life

When we think of play, we think of children playing, but play is also important for adults. Play helps us grow, learn, develop our sense of humor, and explore creativity. It allows us to relax into the moment with enthusiasm and engagement—all key components of self-care. How do you incorporate playfulness in your life? What people or situations make you feel the most playful?

_____

_____

_____

_____

_____

_____

Today, let yourself be a little silly, create something, dance, play a sport, or engage in an activity that makes you smile and laugh. Watch YouTube and dance. Get some playdough or bubbles at the local drugstore. Let yourself enjoy being playful.

———

Allowing play into my life makes
me happy and engaged.

Don't Wish Away Your Emotions—Accept Them

Emotions such as anger, depression, and anxiety can be difficult to manage. But if you can learn to accept those difficult feelings, you're more likely to get through them with relative ease. How do you tend to deal with your overwhelming emotions? Do you tend to wish them away, deny them, react to them, or accept them?

Visualize a beach ball in a body of water. The more you push the beach ball down, the more it resists and is likely to pop up—just like your emotions. The more we suppress our thoughts and deny our feelings, the more they will resurface. Now visualize the ball ebbing and flowing with the water.

I seek to embrace and grow through my difficult emotions, not deny or avoid them.

Acceptance of Others

Learning to accept people despite their differences allows you to be more self-aware and to create an environment where you'll be accepted in return. Who do you need to work on accepting in your life?

_____

_____

_____

_____

_____

_____

_____

_____

Visualize or go outside and feel the rays of the sun piercing through your body, healing you with warmth and lightness. Use this light to warm you with love and acceptance of others in your life, even if you wish they were different.

———————

*I accept others for being themselves
instead of who I want them to be.*

Grief and Self-Care

A painful breakup, estrangement, death of a loved one, or even losing a dream job—all types of loss require insight and sensitivity to work through. Reflect on any loss or grief that you have experienced and how it has affected your self-care.

Where are you right now? Use the five stages of grief to gauge your senses.

- **DENIAL:** "I don't admit that I am or ever was hurt."

- **ANGER:** "I blame others—even life's unfairness—for my hurt."

- **BARGAINING:** "If I act differently, maybe I can change everything."

- **DEPRESSION:** "Regrets consume me, and I cannot live fully in the present."

- **ACCEPTANCE:** "I can grow from the hurt."

Moving through grief helps me heal.

The Healing Process

What do the stages of grief look like in your actions and words? For example, if you are still in a stage of anger about a loss or breakup, does it have a ripple effect in your life in general? How does the stage you are going through manifest itself in your life?

_____

_____

_____

_____

_____

_____

_____

_____

To minimize the ripple effect in other areas of your life, join a support group, open up to someone you trust, look for a therapist, or start a journal. Make a general effort to be more aware of how your stages of grief might be in your day-to-day life.

———————

I can heal from my grief as I move toward the stage of acceptance.

Declutter Your Life

Self-care involves keeping the personal space around you decluttered and organized. If your living space is organized and uncluttered, you're likely to think more clearly and in a more organized way. What things in your living space would you like to change?

_____

_____

_____

_____

_____

_____

_____

_____

Strive to make your living space an *island of peace*. Think of one small step you can take today to spend 5 or 10 minutes declutter-ing your surroundings. Clean out your purse, organize a drawer, or simplify one shelf at a time to declutter.

———————————

An uncluttered and calm physical space
will help calm my inner space, too.

Break Large Goals into Manageable Ones

Let's take decluttering for self-care a step further. Think of a big home project you want to complete. Write down one large task on your to-do list that could benefit from breaking into small steps.

_____

_____

_____

_____

_____

_____

_____

Start on your list today. Make a checklist. Writing down tasks and checking off each one as you complete it is visually satisfying and motivating!

———

Managable steps help me stay on track.

Review and Reflect

Let's take a few moments to reflect on what has meant the most to you in this journal. What prompts, practices, and reflections have helped you the most toward your self-care goals, and why?

_____

_____

_____

_____

_____

_____

_____

_____

Nighttime is perfect for reflecting about your day. Before you go to sleep tonight, review your day and your recent progress in your self-care journal. Make it a nightly habit to identify what's been most helpful to improve your self-care.

Learning from difficult times and challenges make me deeper instead of weaker.

Honor the Mind/Body Connection

Your body and your mind work in sync to take care of you. What ways do you keep physically active while ensuring that self-care is a priority?

Find a way to keep active every day—even a walk around the block will work. Establish a routine to improve your body, your mood, and ultimately your self-care journey.

Keeping active helps me in mind and body.

Have a Growth Mindset

Defining yourself by your successes and failures can lead you to a "fixed mindset." It is much healthier to have a "growth mindset," which stresses effort and perseverance. A "growth mindset" is correlated with higher life satisfaction, allowing you to concentrate on growth and improvement. Do you define yourself too much by your successes or failures? How can concentrating on your growth improve your self-care?

Spend a few minutes outdoors looking around at all the things growing: grass, trees, flowers, plants—they are all in the process of growth. Use this visualization as a way to remind yourself to focus on your own growth mindset.

My effort and growth fuel what I am becoming.

How High You Get Up

"Resiliency" refers to the ability to bounce back from adversity and is directly tied to the ability to handle challenging times. Reflect on times when you demonstrated resiliency and were able to recover from setbacks, perhaps emerging even stronger than before.

_____

_____

_____

_____

_____

_____

_____

_____

Now take that experience and use it to fuel action toward resolving your current self-care challenges. Reflect on the examples of how high you bounced back, not how low you have fallen. Think of one action today to improve your resiliency.

———

I will focus on how I can bounce back.

Pandemic Resiliency

No matter where you are in the world, all of us are joined in facing COVID-19, the invisible enemy. We have all been beset with loss, isolation, anxiety, and disruption of our normal lives in widely varying degrees. It seems safe to say that we all will come out of the pandemic different than we were going into it. How has experiencing the pandemic changed you?

_____

_____

_____

_____

_____

_____

_____

Take a few moments to reflect upon how you have grown through the trauma, loss, and pandemic anxiety. What gifts has experiencing this pandemic given you? What will you never take for granted again?

---

*My resiliency helps me evolve and
grow through this crisis.*

Revisiting Your Spiritual Self-Care

In an earlier prompt (page 16), we focused on the importance of spiritual self-care. Use this time to reflect and revisit the self-care topic here to underscore the importance of connecting with a deep inner sense of purpose that is bigger than yourself. How have you begun to lay a foundation for a better sense of purpose? How have you been nourishing yourself spiritually?

_____

_____

_____

_____

_____

There are many ways to practice spiritual self-care. Organized religion, yoga, meditation, connecting with nature, contemplation, and reading devotions are just some examples of spiritual self-care. For the next four weeks, take up a short practice or ritual every day to connect to your sense of higher power and life's meaning.

My spirituality helps me create meaning in my life.

DATE:

Be Creative

Creativity can help boost your self-care. It can be energizing and motivating, and it allows you to become more free thinking and grow as you actualize your potential. In what ways are you creative, and how would you like to explore your creativity further?

_____

_____

_____

_____

_____

_____

_____

Creativity can take the form of movement, writing, art, crafts, or music, to name a few. Take a painting class with friends or learn a new dance. Start a small garden or write a short story. The goal isn't to create a perfect picture, but rather to enjoy the process of creative expression.

———————

*I take risks and enjoy the process
of creating something new.*

Draw Your Feelings

Consider how you feel in this moment. Are you happy, stressed, or excited? What would those emotions look like? Take a few minutes to express yourself through art. Draw how you feel.

The next time you feel angry, hopeless, or afraid, draw your feelings. You may find that solutions come more quickly or with greater clarity once you express your feelings through drawing.

Creativity opens my world up to new opportunities, feelings, and sensations.

Work Those Muscles!

Muscle strengthening is an important part of maintaining your physical health. Strength training and stretching are all helpful in keeping you heathy, controlling your weight, improving your bone density, and keeping you fit to prevent injury. What do you currently do to strengthen your muscles and tone your body?

_____

_____

_____

_____

_____

_____

_____

Today, spend a few minutes focusing on strengthening your muscles. Squats, sit-ups, stretching, using resistance bands, or doing your favorite conditioning exercises are just a few examples. Commit to this practice at least three times a week for the next month, and it may become a lifelong habit!

Choices that I make for my muscular strength help my general overall health.

Financial Self-Care

Take a moment to evaluate your financial self-care with the following questions: Do you live within your means? Are you stretched too thin and unable to keep to a budget? Do you have a budget? Are you in debt? What would you like to change about your financial habits?

....

....

....

....

....

....

....

....

From your answers above, craft one action item for each change you would like to make in how you handle your financial self-care. As your financial needs and circumstances change, revisit your financial habits frequently to make sure they are working for you and not causing more stress.

----

*My financial health is important
to my total self-care.*

Your Financial Self-Care Goals

As you explore your to-do items in the previous entry, make sure you are not going it alone. All too often, people keep their financial concerns to themselves. Some people even hide them from their partners. Who do you talk to about your finances?

Enlist support to help you identify your financial goals in the short- and long-term. If you want to keep a stricter budget, having someone to hold you accountable will be helpful. Seek out the help of a professional for investment and savings advice.

I am open and honest, and enlist the help that I need to reach my financial self-care goals.

Manage Your Stress

Stress is often characterized as negative. But stress can be quite positive and necessary for a healthy life, and can serve as an indicator that you need change. It can be motivating and create meaning. List at least five ways to finish this sentence: Stress is . . .

Review your list. Put a "+" next to entries that can be viewed as positive and a "–" next to those that are too overwhelming. When you experience stress, make a list of your stressors and do this activity to help you sort through your stress and find ways to embrace it.

Stress motivates me—it does not debilitate me.

Make Beautiful Music with Stress

Managing stress is vital to self-care. It's important to view stress as motivating and positive, not something to be avoided. Stress can even help you grow if you find the right balance. Write some examples of ways that stresses in life have helped you develop positive qualities in yourself.

Visualize someone playing guitar. If a tuning peg is turned too much, its string will snap. If it is not turned enough, the string will be flat. The right amount of tension gives us beautiful music. Reflect on this visualization and how it can inspire you to find your own balance in life to enjoy its beautiful music.

I seek balance to manage my stress.

Post-Traumatic Wisdom

The act of self-care is based on our ability to help soothe ourselves and attend to our own healing from trauma and loss. But this can be tricky to put into action. You may have experienced post-traumatic stress that has made it difficult to move past certain events. Reflect on any losses or traumas you have experienced that have profoundly affected you and have made self-care challenging.

For these losses or traumas, think of how each one has helped you grow and become the person you are today. This is called post-traumatic growth or post-traumatic wisdom. Find the positive things that result from your life circumstances. Think of examples of post-traumatic stress and how you have moved on to post-traumatic wisdom.

My stress is an opportunity
for growth and healing.

Being Social Helps Manage Stress

Connecting with others can help alleviate stress. It's also a part of self-care. Building lasting connections can help you manage stress, as you gain support and realize you are not alone. What are some ways you can best use your connections to manage stress? How does socialization help you manage stress?

Reflect on your most pressing life stresses and who you ask for help, even if it is just to have someone listen. Visualize your stress as a heavy bucket of water that you're trying to hold on to. Now visualize a person you feel connected to helping you carry that same bucket. The load is much lighter, right? If your stresses persist, please seek help from a mental health professional.

I strive to connect and seek
support in times of stress.

Revisit Negative Thinking

Earlier in the book, we addressed the importance of avoiding cognitive distortions (pages 94 and 95). What negative thoughts continue to be the hardest to give up? How have those ANTS affected your behavior and your choices?

One technique for depriving your negative thoughts of so much power is to get bored by them. For example, say the negative thought aloud for two minutes. It is like saying "bread ... bread ... bread ..." for two minutes straight. After a while, the words lose their meaning. Try this anytime you want to get bored with your negative thoughts!

I work hard to stop giving my negative thoughts so much power.

Honor Your Feelings

When we are sad or hurt, it's easy to pretend that everything is just fine. But you have the right to honor your feelings. What are some feelings that you have hidden from others? Have others in your life minimized your feelings? If so, how has that affected you?

Consciously start your self-talk with "I feel" as you go about your day. Whenever you catch yourself thinking about anything at all, look for the feelings attached to the thought. This practice teaches you how to accept your feelings—not judge them. Owning and acknowledging your feelings is an important aspect of emotional self-care.

I honor my feelings;
I have a right to all of them.

Who Are Your Role Models?

Taking stock of who your role models are can help you clarify your own values and choices, which is important for self-care. Think of at least one person you value highly. What about them makes them so important to you? What qualities do they possess?

_____

_____

_____

_____

_____

_____

_____

Instead of comparing yourself to your role models, learn important life lessons from them. Choose at least one value that your role model represents. This could be someone's financial independence (value: stability/success) or the way their smile is genuine and contagious (value: authentic positivity). How can you incorporate those values within yourself?

Important people in my life continue to inspire me and help me better myself.

Have Bigger-than-Yourself Goals

In addition to finding your passions and interests, self-care also requires striving for goals outside of yourself. In what ways do you commit yourself to bigger-than-yourself goals? Examples include volunteering, caretaking, parenting, and helping others in various forms. Reflect on how giving yourself to goals outside of your immediate needs can improve your self-care.

Spending time on important causes adds more meaning to our lives. Contact a volunteer organization, a spiritual or religious group, or a cause you believe in. Remember though, outside involvements should augment your self-care, not replace it.

I commit myself to a sense of purpose much bigger than myself to create my life's meaning.

Choose an Authentic Life

As you've progressed through this book, how has your self-care journey evolved? How has using self-care practices provided new meaning for your authentic self? What has helped you be the best *you*? How have you become more authentically yourself over the course of this journal?

_____

_____

_____

_____

_____

_____

_____

Living a life of authenticity is the foundation of self-care. Sit in a comfortable place and take a few moments to connect to a deeper level within yourself. Tap into your inner strength and core values. Enrich your life as you are guided by your inner wisdom. Trust being who you want to be instead of trying to "measure up" to expectations whether they are your own or those of others.

_To be the best version of me is better
than trying to be like anyone else._

Mindfulness Revisited

In the beginning of this book, we focused on the importance of mindfulness. This is your reminder to revisit the practice of present-centered, nonjudgmental awareness. How has mindful practice impacted you, and what has been a challenge for you to keep mindfulness practice as a way of life?

Today, choose mindfulness in all your activities. Using nonjudgmental awareness, suspend judgments about how things "should be" and just note how they are. Take a mindful walk and notice the beauty around you without thinking the grass should be greener. Look at the flowers around you and appreciate the beauty and uniqueness of each one.

I am committed to a daily practice of acceptance and awe of what I experience in my day.

Making a Self-Care Plan

Think of the most important takeaways that have been helpful in this journal. A good start is to write down at least five self-care goals you have. Creating this list will keep you committed to improving your self-care. What areas do you need to continue to work on?

Look back at your entries and reflect on where you have come from, where you are now, and where you still want to be. Revisit areas in the book that you believe would be useful to process again and add to your entries. What progress have you noticed? Give yourself a figurative pat on the back to acknowledge your effort and progress.

My self-care is a priority.

Revisit Your Self-Help Toolkit

To build on the previous entry (page 146), revisit the notion of a self-care toolkit using various objects to represent your most important self-care practices. If you put together a toolkit earlier, what item from it has been the most helpful to you?

_____

_____

_____

_____

_____

_____

_____

Keep adding to your toolkit when you think of other meaningful objects that represent your self-care goals. For example, a pencil can represent that you're writing the next chapter of your life, or a label can remind you to relabel or revise your negative thinking.

My self-help toolkit
will keep on evolving as I evolve.

Your Turn

We have focused on many aspects of self-care in various realms, including emotional, physical, spiritual, and medical self-care. What area of self-care would you like to develop that may not have been addressed? What could you add to this book? What prompt can you give yourself that would be relevant to you in your self-care journey?

_____

_____

_____

_____

_____

_____

_____

Be creative in continuing on your path to regular self-care. Think of a new question or prompt every day to create a space for reflection, insight, and action. You don't have to have all the answers, but questions and prompts such as the ones you've written here can help you explore what is most meaningful along your self-care path.

_Asking questions, learning, and growing
are a big part of my self-care journey._

A Year from Now

An important part of your self-care journey from here forward will be your self-care vision for yourself. One year from now, what will your self-care practice be like?

Use your answers to propel you forward in using the self-care techniques in this book. Revisit the techniques that resonated deeply with you. You will find that sometimes you relate more to certain entries than others, depending on what is happening in your life. Make a vision board using images you've printed out—or your own words and drawings—to visually represent your self-care goals for the next year.

———

I am committed to self-care—it is the greatest gift I can give to myself and others.

My Self-Care Takeaways

Your commitment to your daily practice of self-care has hopefully enriched your life. If you still have trouble making time for yourself, keep working to carve out moments of self-care every day. What are your most important takeaways from this self-care journal? What has been the most helpful? How has your self-care developed through using this journal?

Even if you completed this book, realize that your self-care journey is never-ending. Every day your commitment to self-care will help you become the best you can be for yourself and others. Consider starting this book again, this time using a separate place to write your responses so you can compare your answers. Review how your answers changed and how you've grown.

My self-care is never-ending.

The thing that is really hard, and really amazing, is giving up on being perfect and beginning the work of becoming yourself.

Anna Quindlen

A FINAL WORD

You did it! Congratulations for choosing to commit time and focus to your self-care. What a gift you have given to yourself and the world around you.

I hope this book has helped you get healthier in mind, body, and spirit. I hope you gained insight into getting in touch with your authentic self, seeking deeper meaning, and making a commitment to being proactive in your health choices. I hope you received the inspiration and insight you needed to make healthy choices for yourself, such as choosing a positive attitude over a negative one, gratitude over bitterness, proactivity over reactivity, resilience over self-defeat, acceptance over judgment, healing over debilitation, forgiveness over grudges, and connection over isolation.

Hopefully, this book will serve as a jump start to making self-care a lifelong priority. If you found particular entries helpful, continue to revisit those prompts, practices, and affirmations to reinforce your growth. Use another notebook and compare your newer responses with your original ones to process how you have evolved. You might even consider going through the entire book again for reinforcement and increased familiarity with important self-care concepts.

Remember never to be apologetic for taking time for yourself. If you do not take care of your own needs and respect them, you will be less likely to spread positivity, kindness, and happiness to the world.

Thank you for allowing me to be your guide along your self-care path. I feel privileged that you have allowed me into your life. Remember to keep moving upward and onward, making yourself a priority. Your commitment to yourself is also a commitment to be the best *you* to those around you. I sincerely wish you unlimited success as you strive to enrich your life and continue your beautiful and meaningful self-care journey!

RESOURCES

BOOKS

The Anxiety and Stress Solution Deck: 55 CBT and Mindfulness Tips and Tools by Judith Belmont

Embrace Your Greatness: 50 Ways to Build Unshakable Self-Esteem by Judith Belmont

Get Out of Your Mind and Into Your Life: The New Acceptance and Commitment Therapy by Steven C. Hayes and Spencer Smith

Learned Optimism: How to Change Your Mind and Your Life by Martin E. P. Seligman

The Self-Care Prescription: Powerful Solutions to Manage Stress, Reduce Anxiety, and Increase Well-Being by Robyn L. Gobin

Self-Compassion: The Proven Power of Being Kind to Yourself by Dr. Kristin Neff

Self-Love Workbook for Women by Megan Logan

The Swiss Cheese Theory of Life by Judith Belmont and Lora Shor

Ten Days to Self-Esteem by David D. Burns

The Upside of Stress: Why Stress is Good for You, and How to Get Good at It by Kelly McGonigal

A Year of Self Esteem: Daily Reflections and Practices for Embracing Your Worth by Judith Belmont

WEBSITES

Belmont Wellness (BelmontWellness.com)
My website offers free self-care and self-help resources such as handouts and worksheets for various mental health and wellness topics.

Lifehack (Lifehack.org)
This site offers a treasure trove of self-help posts to improve your mind and body.

Living Well with Sharon Martin (LiveWellWithSharonMartin. com/mental-health-blog)
Posts about wellness, healing, and emotional self-care.

The Positivity Blog (PositivityBlog.com)
Helps you stay optimistic and motivated and provides inspiration to remain on your self-care mission.

Tiny Buddha (TinyBuddha.com)
The tagline for this site says it all: *Simple wisdom for complex lives.*

REFERENCES

Alberti, Robert E. and Michael L. Emmons. *Your Perfect Right: A Guide to Assertive Behavior*. Oakland, Calif.: Impact Publishers, 1970.

Beattie, Melody. *Codependent No More: How to Stop Controlling Others and Start Caring for Yourself*. Center City, Minn.: Hazelden, Publishing, 1986.

Burns, David D. *Feeling Good: The New Mood Therapy*. New York: William Morrow, 1999.

Doran, G. T. *"There's a S.M.A.R.T. Way to Write Management's Goals and Objectives." Management Review* 70, no. 11 (1981), 35–36.

Dweck, Carol S. *Mindset: The New Psychology of Success*. New York: Ballantine Books, 2007.

Hayes, Steven C. and Spencer Smith. *Get Out of Your Mind and Into Your Life: The New Acceptance and Commitment Therapy*. Oakland, Calif.: New Harbinger, 2005.

Kobasa, S. C. "Stressful Life Events, Personality, and Health: An Inquiry into Hardiness." *Journal of Personality and Social Psychology* 37, no. 1 (January 1979), 1–11. doi org/10.1037/0022-3514.37.1.1.

Kübler-Ross, Elisabeth. *On Death and Dying* (50th Anniversary ed.). New York: Scribner, 2014.

McGonigal, Kelly. *The Upside of Stress: Why Stress is Good for You, and How to Get Good at It*. New York: Avery, 2016.

Neff, Kristin. *Self-Compassion: The Proven Power of Being Kind to Yourself*. New York: William Morrow, 2011.

Acknowledgments

I am truly grateful for my clients over the years who have trusted me to help them on their mental health and emotional wellness journeys. I have learned from them just as they have learned from me, and I appreciate how they have opened their hearts and life stories to me. This has helped me develop the insight and understanding of major life lessons that I impart in my books, which came alive through their examples. I am also thankful to you, my readers, for allowing me to guide you on your self-care journey. It is an honor and a privilege that you have put your faith in me. Thanks also to the talented editors, graphic designers, and staff at Callisto Media, who have provided me with the structure to ensure this book's success.

About the Author

JUDITH BELMONT, MS, graduated from the University of Pennsylvania with a BS in psychology and Hahnemann Medical College of Philadelphia with an MS in clinical psychology. She is the author of 10 mental health and wellness books and two therapeutic card decks. She is a retired licensed psychotherapist and currently offers online mental health coaching, as well as online webinars and workplace wellness presentations at BelmontWellness.com.